Myths Of Being Loved

Meghana Kancharla

Contents

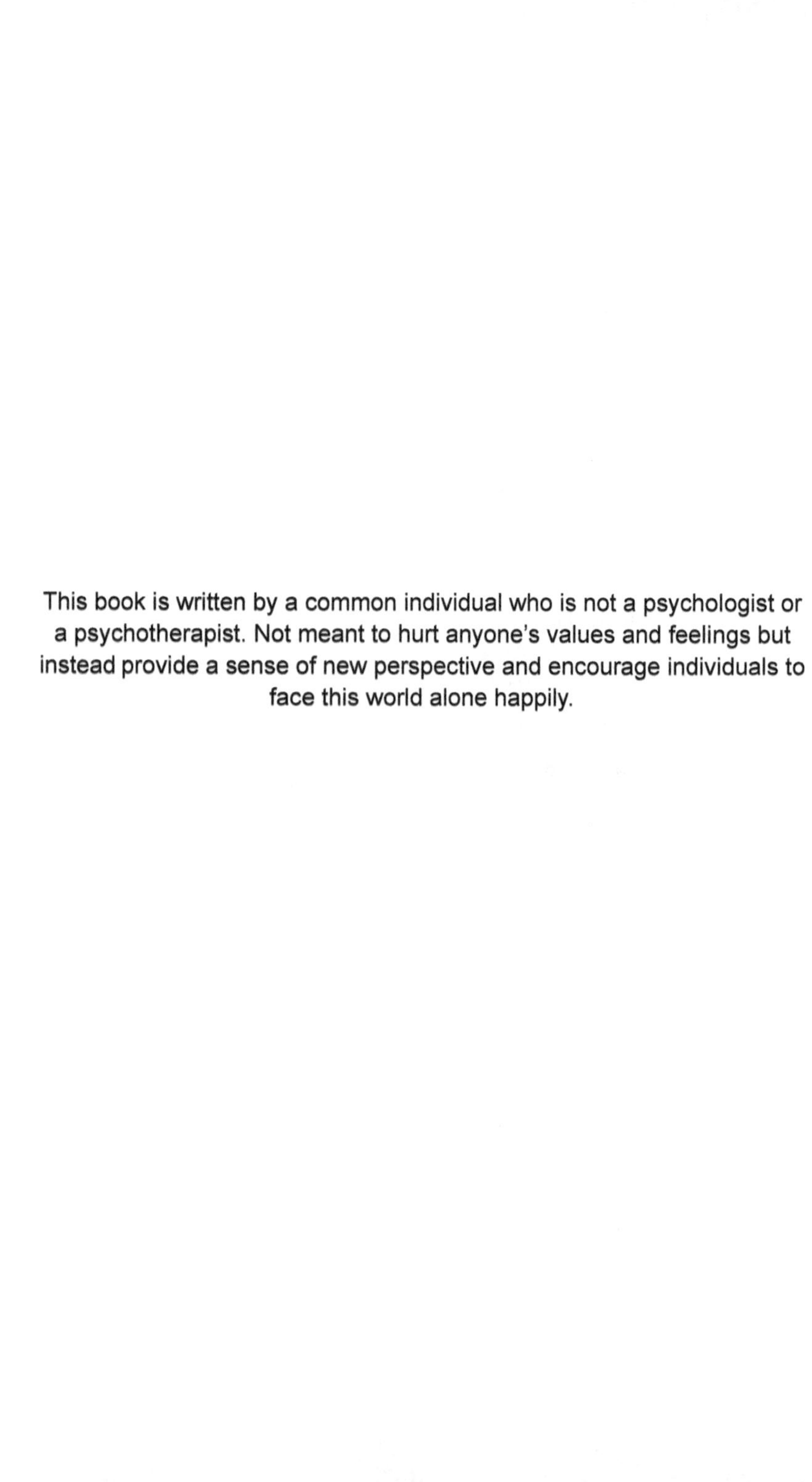

This book is written by a common individual who is not a psychologist or a psychotherapist. Not meant to hurt anyone's values and feelings but instead provide a sense of new perspective and encourage individuals to face this world alone happily.

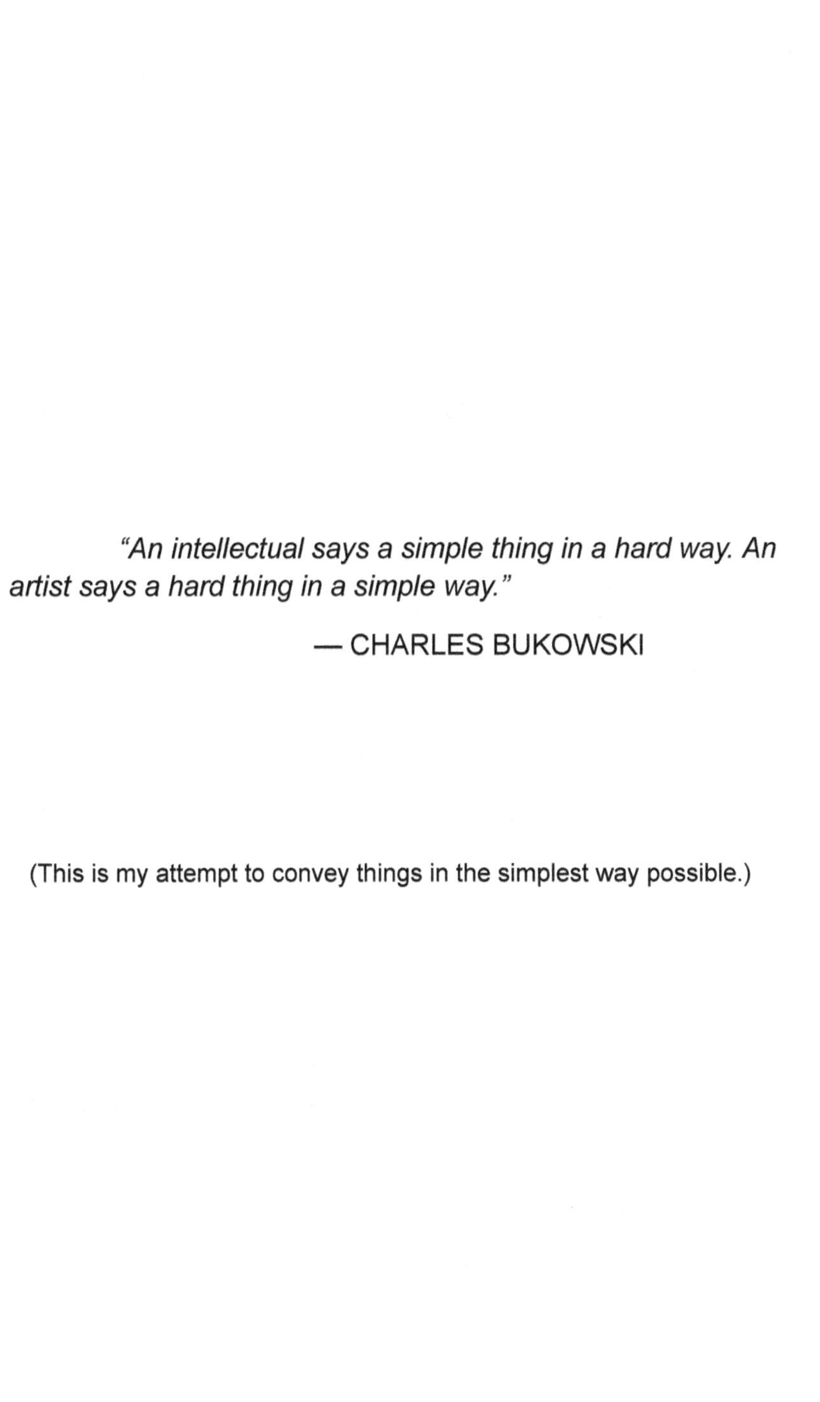

"An intellectual says a simple thing in a hard way. An artist says a hard thing in a simple way."

— CHARLES BUKOWSKI

(This is my attempt to convey things in the simplest way possible.)

1. Chapter One

Some of you may believe that

One tries to learn to be happy alone.

When they go through something distressing,

tragic or downhearted by people around them.

And they are right! Poetry comes from pain.

Maturity comes from misery and

Self-love comes from self-distrust.

Everyone on this planet wants to be loved.

But how many of us are being loved?

One in a hundred, one in a thousand, or one in a million.

What I mean is actually being loved in a way we need, want, and we crave for.

These days, there is no selfless love

Even if it exists, I have certainly not noticed.

We should prepare ourselves so that if someone is pouring love on us,

it simply means they are also expecting something from us in return, for sure.

They must be expecting some attention,

care, and love or, in the worst cases, something offensive.

Many of us have never experienced true love.

Sometimes we get confused by a few words.

a couple of actions and a small amount of attention.

Those short-term delusions result in long-term anxious depression.

We never know others' intentions until they achieve them or fail to hide them.

The whole game starts when we start dreaming

about the beauty of being loved by someone special.

And the saddest truth is that

our generation forgot how to love exactly.

We just try to love someone at times.

However, neither of us knows what it clearly means.

The whole thing became so complicated.

Tell me who is to blame—we ourselves.

We don't want to be loved by everyone.

We just want to be loved by specific people in our lives.

We neglect those who are dying to be with us in a seamless way

and break their hearts, and then. They become heartless.

I am not trying to say we always hurt them intentionally, but we don't realise it.

We have no interest in them.

We are quite busy chasing those who pretend to care about us.

By doing these, are we going to get what we desire?

Of course not, Karma hits back.

And in a world full of heartless people,

How can someone be loved?

There is a famous quote that says,

'To love someone is nothing; to be loved by someone is something; to love someone who loves you is everything.'

Seriously, does loving someone mean nothing?.

In some simple lines, someone expressed their

opinion and we believe them as some kind of fact.

Opinions are meant to be considered, not to be trusted blindly.

Different eyes see different things.

Being able to love is a beautiful thing in this universe.

Being loved by someone deeply may give you the strength

But loving someone deeply gives you courage.

Loving someone adds purpose to life.

We don't have to be loved by someone;

our worth doesn't depend on it.

For instance, imagine a classroom full of students.

How will you decide which student is more valuable?

The student who is good in academics or the one who is bad,

The student who has more friends, or the one with more enemies,

The student who is popular, or the one who is not,

What do you think?

Isn't it ridiculous?

A person's worth is not something

Someone can easily decide and judge.

Every single person is valuable and unique in their own ways.

Let me discuss a very common thing:

Some parents mostly have their favourite kid,

Even if they have only two kids, they must

Select one favourite kid and love them more.

This selection process varies from one another depending on their own theories.

Then sometimes they just randomly try to love us so we don't hate them.

Of course, they love all their children.

But that little unnecessary discrimination is foolishly necessary to make.

Neither of their kids can be benefited.

The one who got all the love wants everyone to just prioritise him and can't handle

being an option in any case, which is not possible practically.

And the one who never experienced more love from their parents

always searches for it everywhere and in everything.

That favourite kid never values their love.

They just enjoy their status uninterrupted.

The other kid, a poor fellow, tries most of his life

just to get prioritised by their parents,

tries to analyse why their parents love their

siblings more and try to prove themselves better.

Isn't it too cruel?

Are they raising someone else's kid or what?

when they can only afford their attention,

love and care for one kid then,

They should have just given birth to one.

Why simply play with their children's mental health?

All of us want to be the dearest children of our parents.

favourite student of our teacher,

best friend of our friends,

first choice for our soulmate, and soon

but the loop of wanting and trying just continues.

At the moment, we get tired of everything.

And even if we get prioritised in a few cases,

It's just a matter of time before

We crave something else.

In the end, everyone thinks they need at least one person to truly love them.

But the problem is,

They are all tired of giving and failing.

They want to receive it first.

Then how will this ice break?.

Even if it does work out,

We want to be loved more than we give love.

By that, I just remembered another insensitive

quote that says that:

'Life is better if we find people who love us more than the people we love more.'

So, do you want to be selfish in love by receiving more?

All this became some kind of business.

Give less and take more;

profits and benefits are essential.

Comparing love with business is not a new thing

But normalising it is a strange thing.

Even if there is some selfless love left in this world,

It's just a matter of time before it completely vanishes.

under the influence of the wrong hands.

Some of you may think you are actually

being loved, but you know what? Just because

You feel loved, that doesn't mean they really love you.

Meanwhile, in some cases, just because you don't feel loved,

doesn't mean they don't love you

It is as difficult as it is to understand the true intentions of the people.

Likewise, understanding our own feelings

and realising the fact that just because

you loved them doesn't mean they felt loved.

Understanding the difference between the way they want to be loved and

The way we do it is the main task,.but unfortunately

we don't put that much effort into it.

Because we want loving them to be a simple task,

We only offer what is easy and comfortable for us in the name of love.

(Still, it is much better than acting like you care when you don't, but just because you like other people's attention.)

We only love to a trouble-free, uncomplicated extent.

But we want to be loved unconditionally, right?

"Life is not about finding yourself. Life is about creating yourself."

— GEORGE BERNARD SHAW

2. Chapter Two

People are normalising making shameful mistakes in a relationship

and expecting another chance or forgiveness like it's nothing.

Even if a person cheats in a relationship,

They want other people to excuse them.

in the tag "accepting each other's flaws.".

Thanks to technology, they can find hundreds of idiotic quotes

that support their deadly faults.

Need an example? Sure.

We often hear people say,

'Right person, wrong time'

It is a better excuse to not blame either.

Just denounce time.

You know the right person will fight for you instead of leaving.

If you think everything in your relationship is perfect,

except the situations around that simply mean

They have to try harder.

If they can't handle you,

then they are not perfect for you.

Even if they met you at the right time and in better situations,

They can't handle you if things go wrong later on.

Don't you need someone who is capable of

loving you even in hard times.

No two people's mindset is exactly similar.

Everyone has their own perspective.

We are generally dividing people nowadays as extroverts,

introverts, and ambiverts, birth-order personalities

First born, second born, last born

But do you think there are any two people

in the same category have the same views?

Not really, maybe some qualities may relate to each other, but not many for sure.

We get this thought that there are many people

like us who feel the same, so we are not wrong.

And our perspective is correct by maybe watching

some Instagram reels or quotes, something like that.

You know what?

A study says that the internet has a 9:1 ratio

of negative advice compared to helpful content,

which can make it hard for individuals to practise self-love.

But dear, if only a few match your point of view,

Does that mean you're wrong?.

A big **NO**!, so don't get judged by such things.

You are born to be yourself.

Not to impress someone.

Not to copy someone.

Not to walk in someone's path.

You can be the way you are until or unless it affects someone.

When we are born, we are all so terrified by this world—

light, noise, people, things, everything.

We open our eyes as wide as possible,

try to understand them, and slowly we absorb them.

We learn from what we see and what we hear.

We believe and behave accordingly.

We are all aware that one individual is made up

of the influence of the world around him.

And we carry a few myths that our ancestors

believed with us, even in this modern lifestyle.

Even today, many girls are growing by

assuming that a prince is going to come and change her world magically.

Men are enforced to believe that they are better creatures than women.

(Fairy tails spoiled all of us.)

Before, people were influenced by

only the people around them.

In this digital world,

what we watch online is more responsible

than people around us, like a movie scene,

a song, a reel, a message, a quote, and the rest.

We generally think that we are brilliant.

We don't get influenced that easily by anyone or anything.

Do you know that?

The more self-help videos you watch online,

the more your mind becomes a mess.

The content on social media greatly influences the views and opinions of people.

Even if we all know that the images we are viewing

In social media is manipulated and filtered.

They can still make us feel insecure about

how we look or what's going on in our own lives.

So we should be careful about

what we are watching and whom we are following

as we choose people around us.

Because it has an equal effect on our lives.

Tell me one thing,

Why do we all want to be loved this desperately?

Like, seriously, who taught us this?

Love has become a mysterious treasure we all search for.

Why do we have to be loved?

I personally asked this question to the people I knew.

Most of them said

to stay by my side in my low times,

to take care of me when I become sick,

to not be alone in this strange world,

to listen something that we can't share with everyone,

to fill the void in our lives,

to pack our lives with better memories,

And the most annoying one is that

I will find out if I was loved by someone.

God, is this an experiment?

What do you think?

Why should we need to be loved?

Whatever someone may say as their reason,

I believe that in this world,

everything has an alternative way.

Don't you think these reasons are nothing but excuses?

Now that love feels like a total myth,

No one clearly knows about it.

But we all assume we need it.

I feel there is nothing wrong with wanting it.

But do we actually need it?

No, not compulsorily. I mean, look around;

Many of us are surviving without it, aren't we?.

We are not satisfied with what we are getting.

We complain about everything.

We dream for more, but life goes on as usual.

By the way, tell me,

Do you deserve to be loved by anyone?.

What are you thinking about? Of course, you do.

Maybe not by someone you wanted

But there will be someone else

who is capable of loving you.

You may not deserve a specific person's love.

because you might have hurt them in an

unforgivable way but you can be loved by

other people. You may not deserve

another chance in other people's lives but

you deserve unlimited chances in your life.

What I am trying to say is that no matter

who you are, how you are, where you are,

or what your past is, you deserve to be loved.

Even a villain should be,

as they have their own story.

All of us are villains, heroes, main leads,

second leads, side characters, supporting characters,

or audiences in someone's life.

That doesn't change anything.

What matters is who you are in your life.

Yesterday you might be arrogant,

today you might be the kindest soul ever, and

tomorrow you may become the rudest one.

And you can be loved every day.

We are all precious in our own way.

Okay, let's say we had to be loved

regardless of all this.

Then, how should we be loved?

How do you want to be loved?

We all have to consider this question, think about it,

and then find out our own desires and have clarity.

"Our greatest freedom is the freedom to choose our attitude."

— VICTOR E. FRANKL

3. Chapter Three

How you want to be loved is up to you.

Make your own rules, your own boundaries,

limits and heights, and make yourself clear.

For that, you first need to know about yourself.

Define what you are, who you are, and

what you want to be.

Accept your blemishes and your darkest secrets.

When you meet a person

You will take time to understand them.

define them by observing, right?

In the same way, understand yourself.

Invest as much time in your own feelings

as you do in others, which helps both your

physical and emotional wellbeing.

What's next?

Now that you know yourself and have clarity about how you want to be loved,

you are all set to be loved by someone.

Let's say you don't want to be loved by others;

That's fine, no worries.

But you can't stop that one person.

That's your self.

You subconsciously love yourself more than anyone else,

So why don't we do it consciously?

Generally, loving someone is a process of a

few steps, like:Knowing them,

relating to them, understanding them,

supporting them, being there for them,

To love them for the way they are.

That will be very easy

if you are trying to love yourself.

We never know what others' intentions are,

but we definitely know ours.

Who can ever know you better than you do?

I believe,

A person can never love others if they can't love themselves first.

A person can never forgive others if they can't forgive themselves.

A person can never understand others if they can't understand themselves.

A person can never truly be kind to others if they are harsh on themselves.

A person can never support others if they discourage themselves and so forth.

So loving yourself consciously is the next step.

How do you love yourself?

You can love others partially but you should

at least love yourself wholeheartedly.

Wholeheartedly, how?

Before that, let's discuss how not to love yourself.

Don't complain too much.

Imagine a friend who always points you out.

discourages you, makes fun of your flaws, insults you most of the time.

And another friend who always

praises you and your existence,

supports you, encourages you, and

takes a stand for you most of the time, regardless of anything.

Which one will you be able to love? Isn't it clear?

So just be your best friend.

Be that miraculous person who never sees your flaws as a weakness,

who doesn't complain about everything.

Instead, own it and try to find a way to make it better.

But remember, it is awesome as it is already.

and there is nothing wrong with trying to upgrade.

Most people spend time on self-criticism

when they are alone.

"Why did I say that? Why did I do that?

Why did I react like that? Why did I behave like that?

Why do I look like this? Why just why?".

Seriously, why not?

Just because you said that, you found out that

It is inappropriate, and you will not say it again.

Likewise, every mistake you made

makes you not repeat it again.

There are some mistakes in life,

which should be learned for your own sake.

You will not learn from such mistakes

unless you do them yourself.

Your biggest enemy and critic is no one else

but **YOU.**

The version you want to be and the real version which exists will always be different.

Stop thinking that there is something wrong with you.

That needs to be fixed.

Our perspective makes it more complicated.

Don't regret anything in your life.

That doesn't do any good.

Accepting your truth is the key to growth.

Just observe, analyse, learn, or accept it and move on from it.

Instead, use that time cuddling yourself.

pampering yourself and taking care of yourself.

Believe me, it feels amazing.

If you start treating yourself like you love yourself so much.

So give it a shot, and you will not regret it.

Treat yourself like your favourite idol.

Become your own fan number one.

 Do a small exercise with yourself by

Just one day, or at least one hour

Try to treat yourself like the person

you admire, respect, or fancy.

At first, you laugh while you idolise yourself.

Then you start comparing yourself with them.

Eventually, you will try to question yourself

What quality or thing made you like them?

Analyse and learn from their lives.

You even deserve to be idolised by yourself.

Remember, you are not less than anyone.

Just imagine that you know yourself.

You defined love in your own way, and

You started falling in love with yourself.

You are treating your soul in a way.

You want to be loved and cared for.

You found your peace, and you feel complete.

Imagine being loved like you dreamed of,

And even better than you expected

By none other than yourself.

No outer person needs to fill you up,

heal your pain, make you laugh,

become your comfort zone or do anything for you.

You already have you.

Isn't it amazing? It is.

A study says that self-love can lead to better mental health, higher self-esteem,

more motivation, and many other evidence-based benefits.

When you genuinely love yourself,

you develop a state of acceptance in your attitude.

Nowadays, many of us are aware of the benefits

of self-love and must have tried it every now and then

but not fully experienced its depth.

Why? Here are the reasons.

Many people treat others badly in the name of self-love.

Loving yourself doesn't mean you can act rudely toward others.

I have seen many people doing this.

but they often end up depressed.

If you get angry at others and argue with them more,

even if you win the argument,

you may satisfy your ego but

you will have to bear with all this stress and tension.

Trust me when you are overthinking.

about situations, people, and the past,

You will lose your charm.

Try to achieve peace of mind.

Calm your mind and ease your temper.

Healing is choosing peace over revenge.

Self-love can only be achieved

when you start being kind.

Our generation thinks that just by saying a few nice things,

giving a compliment, replying fast, not being mean,

consoling others, and the rest are acts of kindness.

By doing such things, we consider ourselves kind and good beings.

It's way more than that.

Here, the small gestures are not undervalued,

but by doing such things, one should not consider

themselves that they are doing favours to others and

definitely not expecting anything in return.

You don't have to love them or please them.

But being polite is the bare minimum.

The logic is simple:

When you are kind to yourself,

You don't expect anything in return.

Similarly, when you are being kind to others,

Expect nothing.

Just smile and be your purest self.

With small gestures and a little positivity, embrace yourself slowly.

The key is that loving yourself and being kind to mankind are two consecutive steps.

They should be balanced in order to achieve self-love.

If you are doing only one thing then you're being selfish.

Many develop a mindset like,

'Yaar, from today I will prioritise myself; I won't give a shit about others; I will be a completely different person'.

No, you don't have to be a completely different person.

You don't have to change your behaviour overnight. It doesn't work like that.

Life doesn't change magically one day.

Instead, make it a habit.

A slow habit

Try to be the best version of yourself;

don't erase the previous version.

"Today is yours to shape. Create a masterpiece!"

— STEVE MARABOLI

4. Chapter Four

Nowadays people are represented as flags

red flag, green flag and others.

But in real life we are all colour blind or

we can't identify the true colours of people rapidly

It takes time and tasks to discover them.

People simply define the things they can't tolerate as red flags.

How do you define people?

Based on their past activities,

present, or scope of future because

people can change periodically.

Today's man full red flags can turn into a

green forest someday. Viceversa

A man is capable of anything.

Situations, people and time changes people

So we cannot actually define or judge anyone.

All we can do is check whether or not

we can handle them in our life.

Cause at the end of the day

the only thing that matters is

making life more pleasant.

We always crave things that are beyond our control.

And neglect those that are just in our control.

Do you know that?

Every time you fake a smile,

Regardless of your actual emotions,

Your brain subconsciously believes that you are actually smiling.

It produces endorphins, happy enzymes.

When our brain feels happy, we smile.

When we smile, our brain feels happier.

Our brain is such an innocent fool.

It has no idea about faking a smile.

Take care of that fool!

They say, *Fake it till you make it.*

If you want to be happy, just smile.

If you don't want to fake it, it's okay.

Be with someone who makes you smile often.

Or be someone who knows how to smile often

Do the things that make you feel alive.

Stress will always exist in our lives.

The point is knowing how to handle it.

In every situation, you always have a choice in how you respond.

We always underestimate ourselves.

We can have anything and everything we want.

With our mind, which is the strongest weapon we ever need.

We can do wonders with that.

Only if we wanted to,

Only if we believe in it,

Only if we use it

Knowing something doesn't make you powerful.

Until we use it with faith.

I honestly don't understand why,

Do people assume that

It is okay to hurt other people, when they are upset.

Even though they have nothing to do with you being upset.

They might have tried to make you feel better.

Or they might have regularly approached you.

without knowing that you were upset.

What a world we are living in!

You may not have the courage to deal with your emotions.

But you have the audacity to injure the innocent.

You must be thinking that you don't do such things.

Didn't you ever yell at your mother?

Because you were stressed at work,

You had a fight with someone,

Your superior insulted you,

Or you just had a really bad day.

You are aware that your mother has nothing to do with any of it,

Still, you scream at her.

Since you are aware of the fact that

She loves you,

She will never leave you.

And she will still try to understand you.

So you take her for granted.

That's so nice of you, right?

(If not your parents, then your spouse, siblings, or a friend.)

In some situations, other people don't have to necessarily love you.

If you just estimate that

They are weaker than you.

that they will let you shout, or

that they will let you win the argument.

You will remove your frustration on them.

You can just throw a sorry on their face later on.

People shoot dirt at others in the process of hiding their scars.

For some reason it makes them feel better.

You might be hurt because of something reasonable.

But you don't have any right to damage other people's feelings.

Remember, you are not greater than anyone else.

And the best part is some people say that

'We only get angry at the people we care about'

Excuse me, please, but this is the most foolish thing.

Someone can ever say.

If you love them, get angry at them for their sake.

For their better life,

For their well-being,

Not because you are angry!

That is not the love or care you are pouring on them.

Don't cause the pain,

Because you know how much it hurts.

The way you treat them,

The way you make them feel about you and themselves

Is more important than how much you love them.

What is the point of having such love which brings more tears and misery

than joy and delight.

Even a plant needs water regularly.

If you didn't supply its basic needs to survive,

still love it as it provides you with flowers or other

Adds new shine to your balcony,

You sincerely hope it stays healthy and happy.

And sometimes you just throw trash on it.

Not every time; sometimes when you are upset

Will the plant be alive? How long?

Aren't any relationships similar?

"Yesterday I was clever, so I wanted to change the world. Today I am wise, so I am changing myself."

- RUMI

5. Chapter Five

Our generation is the most silent generation.

All the chaos is present in our minds.

We often space out,

We are all lost in our own thoughts.

Our imagination, our delusions,

our fears, our doubts, and our pain.

We all mostly forget to live in the moment.

Occasionally, we try to live in the moment.

Like some special moments or celebrations.

Though we seem toxic to our elder generation,

We were just toxic to ourselves, more than to any other people.

People even started taking their revenge on social media.

Most of the fights happen there.

In the war called chatting,

We strike other people with our text messages as if it is our sword.

Leaving unseen and on seen are exclusive position of attacks.

We end the war temporarily or permanently.

With a time-bomb called 'block' button.

Some are even like,

'Okay, you hurt me now. I will see you online tonight.'

We say a few things on social media which

we will never be able to say directly face-to-face.

We act much more rudely online than offline.

As if wifi is on, humanity is off.

Being called 'heartless' and 'cold'

are taken as some compliments.

Genz totally has a different dictionary.

From fake crying in front of our parents,

Cause everyone cares.

To fake smiling in front of society, no one cares.

We all grew up.

This is the era where people feel

Awkward when others cry

Instead of being worried

We hear people saying this the most

That they don't know how to console others

As if it was something we were unaware of.

It's just a common emotion.

That we all go through In our low times.

For those who honestly believe

They don't know how to console others.

Slow down; you don't have to do any magic.

to remove their sorrow.

Just try to be available for them.

Try to make them feel that you are there for them.

Listen if they open up.

Tell those routine dialogues

It's okay,everything will be alright.

which has amazing power.

Or similar soothing words

If possible, maintain some physical contact.

By holding them or their hand,

Spread your energy to them

Provide the comfort they need.

Some like privacy, and some like company.

Make sure you provide what they are comfortable with.

 But before you do any of these

Try to truly respect their emotions and feelings.

Empathy is the basic human nature to possess.

I always wanted someone like me in my life.

Someone who loves me as much as I do (to others)

Someone who cares for me as much as I do

Someone who is kind to me as I am

Someone who tries to understand me as I do

Someone who forgives my mistakes as I do

Someone who gets angry at me but never leaves me

Someone who stands for me in the hard times

Someone who never gives up on me when I am upset

Someone who loves me every day

Someone who cries for me when I disappear

Someone who never gets bored of me

Someone who tries all possible ways to make me

smile, like I do to others

I wish I had someone like me in my life.

Is it too much to ask for? I don't know

Then one day I decided to become that someone in my life. And I did.

You can also become that someone in your life.

You always wanted to.

Also make your heart a little bigger and treat others the way you want to be treated without expecting anything in return.

If Love is an art, then be your own artist.

Thank you for reading!

www.ingramcontent.com/pod-product-compliance
Lightning Source LLC
Chambersburg PA
CBHW021756150726
47989CB00004B/1682